Basic Skills

Story Elements

Learning About the Components of Stories to Deepen Comprehension

Grades 5-6

By
Norm Sneller

Cover Artist
Laura Zarrin

Inside Illustrations by
Rebecca Waske

Published by Instructional Fair • TS Denison
an imprint of

 **McGraw-Hill**
Children's Publishing

About the Author

Norm Sneller has taught in elementary school settings for the past twenty-three years. He gained his teaching experience in the United States, Canada, and Honduras. Norm holds a bachelor's degree in elementary education from Calvin College and a master's degree in curriculum and instruction from Michigan State University. He has written numerous books for McGraw-Hill Children's Publishing.

Credits

Author: Norm Sneller

Cover Artist: Laura Zarrin

Cover Design: Matthew Van Zomeren

Inside Illustrations: Rebecca Waske

Project Director/Editor: Kathryn Wheeler

Editors: Mary Hassinger, Linda Triemstra,
            Stephanie Dekker

Graphic Layout: Tracy L. Wesorick

McGraw-Hill
Children's Publishing

A Division of The McGraw·Hill Companies

Published by Instructional Fair • TS Denison
An imprint of McGraw-Hill Children's Publishing
Copyright © 2001 McGraw-Hill Children's Publishing

Send all inquiries to:
McGraw-Hill Children's Publishing
3195 Wilson Drive NW
Grand Rapids, Michigan 49544

Story Elements—grades 5-6
ISBN: 0-7424-0104-9

About the Book

In this book, the elements necessary to critique and discuss a story are reviewed. Teachers, parents, and students who read through the pages of this workbook are encouraged to consider such literary elements as genre, character, setting, action, plot, subplot, climax, point of view, and conflict/problem.

Pages from this book can be used individually to strengthen the recognition of a specific element, or to introduce it as a topic. Workbook activities can also act as springboards prior to creative writing sessions. Teachers might want to use certain pages on more difficult concepts—such as point of view—to help review the material after it has been worked on in class.

Table of Contents

genre

Write Now

Genre means a type of book with characteristics you can recognize. Biographies, science fiction, poetry, and fantasy are all examples of genres. Circle the correct answer to identify each genre.

1. A story set on another planet would probably be

   science fiction   biography   historical fiction

2. A book of haiku written in the fifteenth century would be

   drama   poetry   adventure

3. A book set in New Orleans during the American Civil War would most likely be

   fairy tale   fantasy   historical fiction

4. A book about the life of Martin Luther King Jr. would be

   poetry   biography   mystery

5. A book with talking animals as characters would probably be

   biography   adventure   folktale

Write the genre next to each title.

6. *Cinderella* _____

7. *Middle School on Mars* _____

8. *The Life of Sitting Bull* _____

9. *The Knight and the Dragon* _____

10. *Rhymes for All Seasons* _____

What Genre?

Below are four paragraphs. Each one represents a particular type of writing. Read each selection and circle its **genre**.

1. I hopped on the magne-van after my group meeting at the Edu-plex. We had met to discuss our group research, entitled "Foods Across the Galaxies." We could have met by video phone, but our mentor, Sean Wang, suggested that we share the same space. So now I'm riding in this magne-van, zipping along exactly 15 cm above the flat surface of the Gobi Desert.

   Circle one: fantasy   realistic fiction   historical fiction   science fiction

2. Grandpa held me in his arms as his wings lifted us over the forest. "It's OK, Petey. I won't let go." I just had to cry, so I pressed my face into Grandpa's shoulder and wept softly. My father and mother were missing, and not even the Forest People could find them. I could tell we were slowing down and dropping steadily. "Almost home," murmured Grandpa. We landed in front of our clan's tree home.

   Circle one: fantasy   realistic fiction   historical fiction   science fiction

3. Pa handed me the musket. "Jesse," he mumbled, "You have to get some game for your ma. This leg will keep me down for a spell, I reckon." Pa winced from the pain and set himself down once more on the stool before the fireplace. "I'm counting on you, Jesse. Don't let your ma down, son."

   Circle one: fantasy   realistic fiction   historical fiction   science fiction

4. I want nothing to do with the flower store! Mom's business was good for her...and good for our whole family. But I want to work at the art gallery. Mrs. Fleming suggested that I assist her with her Saturday morning class. Those small children are so much fun to teach. In the afternoons, I could continue my research on Winslow Homer. But Mom wants me to help her. I just don't know what to do.

   Circle one: fantasy   realistic fiction   historical fiction   science fiction

genre

What Is It?

Read the paragraphs. Label each by its genre.
Choose from biography, myth, tall tale, realistic fiction, and science fiction.

When Daniel Boone was a child, he came down with smallpox. We're told he got tired of playing outside when all his brothers were sick in bed. So he sneaked into bed with them. A few days later, Daniel got the pox. His mother was angry—and scared.

1. _____

Why, our winters got so cold the lakes would freeze in minutes. That's how Lost Lake vanished. You see, a large—or rather, gigantic—flock of geese settled down upon it and their feet froze in the water in short order. When they flew off the following morning, they took the whole lake with them.

2. _____

Ida looked at the girl who stood in the doorway. She was her double! She might as well be looking into a mirror. There was no difference in face, form, coloring, even stance. But could this be her clone? No. It couldn't be! That Doctor Enselmeier! He must have perfected his cell enhancer project.

3. _____

All three boys spun out on their bikes, gravel flying. School was out! Ted, in the lead as always, headed toward the park. Pumping hard, the boys tore up Skinflint Hill, through the sandlot, and across the ballpark, slamming on their brakes just shy of the bleachers.

4. _____

"Whatever you do, do not open the box, my dear."
But Pandora, sorely tempted, marveled at the box before her. In a fit of curiosity, she tipped up the lid. Out came the demons of hatred, anger, jealousy, sloth, misery, and treachery. They were followed by others whose sudden escape caused Pandora to flee in terror.
And so evil came to humankind.

5. _____

By the time Zach was five, he had grown to six feet, eight inches. His appetite was so great that his dad worked twelve hours a day just to provide Zach's meals. His voice had deepened, though he still carried a blanket and sucked his thumb. The blanket he adored was a twenty-pound quilt he had made him-self from llama skins.

6. _____

Name _____

character

I Have You Pegged

Sometimes even a name will give a clue about a character.
Match each name with the most likely character description.

1. ____ Pip Skweek   4. ____ Ardie Potter
2. ____ Melodie deForte   5. ____ Lollie Popp
3. ____ Barney Greenfield   6. ____ Ripp Kord

a.   ceramic-loving artist whose pottery can be viewed at the Civic Center
b.   hog farmer from north-central Iowa
c.   four-year-old girl who clings to adults, dirtying their clothes with her sticky hands
d.   young music teacher whose specialty is vocal instruction
e.   stunt man whose parachute jumps are ranked highly in northern British Columbia
f.   small, timid child, unable to defend himself

7. ____ Tex Westing   10. ____ Willow Whirling
8. ____ Stretch VanderHoop   11. ____ Auntie Pasta
9. ____ Clare Vista   12. ____ Willie Phawl

g.   perhaps the most accident-prone person ever to reside in Portland, Oregon
h.   blonde-haired basketball star out of Modesto, California
i.   horse-loving cowhand; wishes he lived 120 years ago
j.   window washer whose work keeps her busy in Manhattan
k.   a slender ballerina with long legs; always wears black leotards
l.   grandmotherly spaghetti maker, formerly from Sicily

Create a name for each of the people listed below:

13. dog catcher _____   16. firefighter _____

14. train engineer _____ 17. golf pro _____

15. state senator _____   18. mall Santa _____

character

Math Madness

Use the grid to discover each character's favorite math topic.

Mr. Warner's math class is great; all his students agree. Whether they measure the length of plants in the classroom, punch keys on their calculators, or create pictographs of world-culture data, they have a blast. Yet, each student in Agate Group has a different favorite topic (one is division). From the clues below, can you determine which topic each student (one is Tomas) likes most and the order in which Agate Group planned out the five math topics?

Use the chart below to help you find the answers.

1. Shenee's favorite topic came sometime after decimal skills were discussed.
2. Neither Li nor Hanna found graphing and geometry to be their most enjoyable topics.
3. Geometry was practiced first. Decimals were learned before Hanna's favorite, which came before ratios.
4. Charting was not taught last. Markos, who loves geometry, was happy that his favorite topic came three before Shenee's.
5. The decimal lover has a five-letter name.

	Division	Ratios	Decimals	Graphs & Charts	Geometry	1	2	3	4	5
Shenee										
Li										
Markos										
Hanna										
Tomas										
1										
2										
3										
4										
5										

$20 \div 4 =$

Name _____

He Said, She Said

Howie Hunter, student sleuth, has eavesdropped
on the ten people listed below. Match each person with the
recordings that Howie made of their conversations.

Suspicious People List

a. Lance Perry, an actor
b. Sharmain Steele, a registered nurse
c. Felix Brecht, a composer of music
d. Bitsy Floss, a patriotic seamstress
e. Lee Deezine, a toy designer

f. Goldie Grahame, a nutritionist
g. Bill Gelbrefe, an attorney
h. Belem El Sher, an exporter
i. Robbie Hollingsworth, a teacher
j. "Lead Foot" LaRue, a trucker

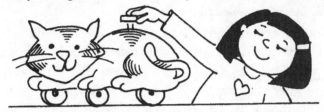

1. ____ "Shall I administer another IV? The patient is asking for one."

2. ____ "Well, I prefer creating fun for kids. Take this Clyde the Cat model, for instance. It always lands on its feet. See?"

3. ____ "Your son is a delight in my room. Yes, I agree...he does have a strong interest in chewing pencils."

4. ____ "How's my hair? Are you ready to shoot? No, I don't need a stunt man for this scene!"

5. ____ "No! Soda should never be substituted for fruit juice! Really!"

6. ____ "Hello, Operator. I'm dialing Paris. Hello, Jacques! Your Persian rugs are ready for shipment. I think you will be delighted."

7. ____ "Ouch! Poked myself again! Yes, dear. I should try to slow down. Now hush and let me finish this star design."

8. ____ "Get off the road, Gramps! You're slowing me down, and this delivery is late!"

9. ____ "First the flutes carry the melody. Then it is taken up by the violins."

10. ____ "No, your Honor. That is not my motion. My client doesn't understand your question."

character

Knowing How to See

Read the selection about Leonardo da Vinci.
Then answer the questions on page 11.

(1) Ah, Leonardo! My master. My teacher. You have come to ask of this great man? Let me tell you what I know.

(2) First, you should know that he never tired of learning. A gifted artist, Leonardo was eager to learn about mathematics, mechanics, architecture, and anatomy. He constantly sketched in notebooks. His sketches were his best notes, the "writing" of his fertile mind.

(3) Beautiful too were his writings, which filled in the spaces among his sketches. (I should know. He left them in my keeping!) These were written in mirror image. It is true! He wrote in reversed form. You might say it was Leonardo's secret code, though it truly was not very secretive. Because my master was left-handed, his writing flowed most easily from right to left.

(4) Leonardo's genius cannot be measured merely by what he accomplished. Oh, no! One must include the many ideas, sculptures, paintings, and inventions he promoted but never completed. Many of his paintings, some for which he was commissioned, were unfinished. His sixteen-foot-high statue of a horse, planned with great detail as a memorial to the founder of the Sforza family, took twelve years of da Vinci's time, but it was never finished. The metal for the statue, hoarded for its casting, was used to manufacture cannons for a war which my master's sponsor lost.

(5) To Leonardo da Vinci, the most important of the five senses was the gift of sight. His goal for himself and for us, his pupils, was "to know how to see," or *saper vedere*. To this end he questioned us constantly and thoroughly on what we recalled of our daily sightings. He encouraged us to detail these images in sketches.

(6) I was invited along with other young artists to join Leonardo in his last years of life. I traveled with him from court to court in the service of various dukes and kings. Because he was gifted in imagining weapons of war, our world considered Leonardo a highly desired resource. Yet, it is his research in the sciences which I have found most fascinating. While with my master, I traveled from Milan to Rome and on to Cloux in France. Everywhere we went, my master was honored and respected by those in whose service he worked. To the French king, Leonardo was "first painter, architect, and mechanic to the King." Yet, my master was permitted to do and to learn as he pleased. He died at the age of 67 in France.

Leonardo's humble student,

Francesco Melzi

Francesco Melzi

Knowing How to See (cont.)

1. Who is the speaker in this selection? _____

2. On which continent does the writer live? (circle your choice)

   North America   Asia   Europe   Africa   South America

3. What question was the writer supposedly asked at the start of the selection? _____

   _____

4. What is the main idea of each paragraph below?

   Paragraph 2 _____

   _____

   Paragraph 3 _____

   _____

   Paragraph 4 _____

   _____

   Paragraph 5 _____

   _____

5. What does the author believe to be Leonardo da Vinci's greatest achievement? _____

   _____

6. What does the phrase *saper vedere* mean? _____

   _____

7. What did da Vinci encourage his students to do to help them see and remember details?

   _____

   _____

Name _____

character

Welcome to Our Assembly

Match each one of the statements overheard
in a school assembly to the correct student.
Pay attention to the character descriptions.

a. Tony Brown: very nervous

b. Abby McMann: observant

c. Percy Pennyfeather: nosy; a busybody

d. Nadia Kosak: arrogant; scheming

e. Jodhi Amani: relieved

f. Jamal Davis: disappointed

g. Mary Marshall: serious; in charge

h. Chang Lee: hopeful; talented

1. ____ "Quiet down, students! We have something important to discuss. I need your attention."

2. ____ "Oh, no! Do you think this is about that prank we pulled at recess?"

3. ____ "Never! We are much too smart to ever get caught!"

4. ____ "That's what you think! I heard *all* about your trick in the hall! You are in BIG trouble."

5. ____ "I think this is about that science award. I think I could win. My project turned out well."

6. ____ "Look! There's that new teacher. I bet this assembly is to welcome her."

7. ____ "Whew! That was close, you guys! It's good that you didn't get caught."

8. ____ "I thought Chang was going to get that award today. Too bad!"

Name _____

Close Inspection

Read the four quotes below and answer the questions that follow.

1. "Hannah, you may have Abby, Blanca, and Courtney come for a sleepover," Dad said, agreeing to his daughter's request.

   a. To whom is the speaker talking? _____

   b. How many girls may come over? _____

   c. What is the daughter's name? _____

   d. Who is the speaker? _____

2. "Ike, if George can't answer the question, Harry will be the next champion," announced Jerry.

   e. Will Jerry be the next champion? _____

   f. Who is the speaker? _____

   g. Must Ike answer the question? _____

   h. Could Harry be the next champion? _____

3. "When Michael was a mere boy, Nan," began Otis, "he and Portia fished at Quincy's Pond not far from Randy's house."

   i. Who went fishing? _____

   j. Who lived near the pond? _____

   k. Did Nan go fishing with Michael? _____

   l. Who is the speaker? _____

4. "It happened that in the reign of Emperor Xaviar of Zelnod, a law was passed by Lord Vilma that all Utentots must leave Trivoli and move to Abundia," began Roland.

   m. Who had to leave? _____

   n. Who demanded that the Utentots leave? _____

   o. When was this law passed? _____

   p. From what town were the travelers to leave? _____

character

I Have a Feeling

Below are eight events. Read them and answer the questions that follow.

a. Faster and fleeter than ever before, Lonnie Lorenzo ran through the trees of the city park. None of the other students could catch him. Today, he was in a league of his own.

b. She swept into the brightly lit hall, aloof and single-minded. This was her day! Lady Beatrice had ordered all her lords to arrive today for a renewal of their oaths of loyalty and, by the Golden Scepter, they had better obey!

c. Eighty-seven-year-old Dorothy Wells, stoop-shouldered from life's work, stepped out onto her porch and scowled at the carload of noisy, rude men parked in front of her house.

d. He looked out, shivering with fear. The fox had followed him to his nest. The young deer mouse pulled back into the shadows.

e. Oh, did his toe ever hurt! Steven hobbled ruefully over to a chair to look his big toe. He had pretended to kick his friend Jeremy. Instead, he had kicked the wall. Steven winced as he pulled off his sock.

f. Ned Tuttle climbed into the back seat with the enthusiasm of a seven-year-old going to the beach. Today he was having those braces removed from his teeth!

g. Helene stared at the diving board. Yes, thirty years ago she would have dared to try it. More than that! She would have excelled! But not now. Her seventy-two-year-old bones ached at the mere thought of diving.

h. Terry yanked the small package from under the decorated tree and tore off the wrapping. "Hey! This not the doll I wanted! Mama!" she yelled.

1. Who is excited about the future? _____

2. Who seems ready for a confrontation? _____

3. Who is the most upset? _____

4. Who has a soaring spirit? _____

5. Who is tired and nostalgic? _____

6. Who is experiencing fear? _____

7. Who appears arrogant and determined? _____

8. Who is sorry for a mistake? _____

setting

Summer Camp

Read the story. Then answer the questions on page 16.

Our camp is great. A bunch of kids from school go there, but I especially like getting to meet the kids from the other schools. We sing crazy songs in the dining hall every noon. There are activities and challenges to try out all day long. The counselors are great, the buildings are clean and airy, and the food is better than some of the meals I get at home.

This year I got Keesha for a counselor. She is so funny! She gets all us girls rolling on the cabin floor laughing at her silly, scary stories at bedtime. But she is smart too. She knows when one of us is homesick or feeling bad. She never pokes fun of us when we do something stupid. And she shows us how to express kindness to the others in our cabin.

Keesha loves nature. She often points out the wildlife in camp. On our second morning of camp, Keesha raced outside as if there were a bee down her back. She yelled something about the witching hour. I always thought that the witching hour was at midnight. We all

thought she had gone off the deep end. Keesha rushed over to a beech tree. The elephant-like trunk had a big hole in it where a woodpecker had hammered out a home. Our counselor reached her hands into the hole and pulled out a young possum. It chittered and squeaked until it saw us kids. Then it pretended to be asleep!

One night, she took all ten of us for a hike through the woods. She warned us to be quiet and to leave our flashlights at the cabin. We walked for maybe twenty minutes when we stopped suddenly. We heard some chattering creatures off to our right. Down by the lake were two raccoons fighting over some bread they had found. They almost sounded like two children squabbling over a treat.

One rainy day, we chose to go deep into state forest land with binoculars, guidebooks, insect repellent, and snack food. We sketched some of the wonderful flowering plants. Keesha knew the history and medicinal value of many of these plants. She showed us one plant which, when broken open, gave off a very powerful smell. She told us it would keep flies and mosquitoes away. I sure could tell why that one would work!

Every evening after supper we'd play games with a whole group of cabins. Keesha volunteered to have our cabin set up the evening game on our fifth day. We walked all over the camp, setting clues for a treasure hunt. This meant that we had to canoe to different landmarks around the lake, crawl under some of the older cabins, plan obscure hiding spots "that everyone should have known about," and race down the camp trails. Of course, we ran out of time. When the bell rang for supper, we were still far across the

Summer Camp (cont.)

field. In our giggle-filled mad dash to the dining hall, we waded through some tall grass. My new friend, Rita, unknowingly stepped over a light blue-gray snake. It was huge! Keesha said it was called a blue racer. We all stood back and watched it, talking quietly. "Look how long it is," said Keesha. "It must be as long as I am!" We watched as the startled snake started to move slowly past us, and then suddenly raced away. We were late for supper that day, but it didn't matter.

I want to go back to camp next summer. I want to know as much about nature as Keesha does. I can dream, can't I?

Answer the questions about the story "Summer Camp."

1. List the two main elements of the setting.

Time: _____ Place: _____

2. Match the specific setting elements with these events by drawing lines to connect.

EVENT	PLACE	TIME
see baby possum	in field	every noon
sing songs	by beech tree	rainy day
discover blue racer	in woods	bedtime
sketch plant specimens	in dining hall	second day
hear scary stories	in state forest land	one night
observe raccoons	in cabin	fifth day

3. Describe the summer camp by discussing the various activities of the campers. _____

_____

_____

_____

_____

_____

setting

In Perspective

Match each quote with the correct setting.

1. "Not much happening here. Wonder if the other side is any busier."

a. _____ a treetop during a windstorm

2. "Who is that fool stomping over my head? It's enough to give me a headache!"

b. _____ on the shore of a deserted island off the coast of Greenland in late autumn

3. "Who told Tommy to buy me a lava lamp? Honestly!"

c. _____ in a science class on a warm spring day

4. "Whoa! This swaying is making me seasick."

d. _____ under a bridge which three goats tried to cross once upon a time

5. "If an object...falls at...a constant rate...of...speed... how-w-w...zzzzzz."

e. _____ standing in the return line the day after Christmas

Describe settings at which these five quotations would be heard. As you give the setting, be sure to describe the time and place.

6. "So what? I think my hair looks ...special." _____

7. "You took *what* with you to the party?" _____

8. "Waah! I don't want to! You can't make me!" _____

9. "He's coming this way. Yes. I see him now." _____

10. "Honey, you shouldn't have!" _____

setting

Another Place

Read the story. Then answer the questions on page 19.

Hello. My name is Ansal Khamba. I am twelve years old and attend a school in the city of Calcutta, India. My parents are both teachers. My father teaches Western literature in a college. If you are American, you might call this a "high school." My mother teaches world studies at the university. Both of my parents have gone to school in other countries as well as India. They've been to Cambridge, England; Cairo, Egypt; Boston, United States; and Bonn, Germany. They say I may go to school overseas if I want. I think I'll stay in India. We have many good universities.

My mother says I should tell you something about our country of *Bharat*. That is the official name of India. It would be difficult to tell you briefly about our country. It is very old and has at least 5,000 years of recorded history. Perhaps I will tell you about some of our beautiful sights instead.

My favorite place is the Taj Mahal. My parents took me there when I was seven years old. This magnificent structure is really a *mausoleum*, a building which houses the bodies of the dead. The towers and spire of the Taj rise high into the sky. An emperor named Shah Jahan ordered this building be created to honor his dead wife, Mumtaz Mahal. Twenty thousand workers worked twenty years to build this memorial, using white marble and red sandstone. They built reflecting pools and gardens outside. Inside, there is an ornate burial chamber where the emperor and his wife are now buried together.

When I was eight years old, my mother took me on a trip to the Bandhavgarh National Park. She said it was for my educational training. The many birds of the park are beautiful. I loved the blues and greens of the peacock and the tinge of pink on the rosy pastor. Still, the park is most famous for the care and protection it offers to tigers. Before the park was expanded, it had more tigers per square kilometer than any other park in the world.

Two years ago, Father and Mother took me to the Thar Desert. What a harsh place! I cannot imagine anyone living in a land like that, yet we saw ancient temples and palaces. We traveled by safari, riding on camels. My camel, whose translated name meant "Stubborn and Foolish," was slow, single-minded, and mean. He spit on people, especially on Kogi, our guide's assistant.

This year, we traveled into the Ladakh. We toured the headwaters of the Indus River. We stayed in the home of a Tibetan refugee family who were gracious hosts. After spending four days getting used to the high altitude, we hiked into the Zaskar Mountains. What a breathtaking view from so high up! We could look down across valleys of terraced fields and villages. Father and Mother also let me visit a nearby monastery called a *gompa*. Buddhist monasteries like the one I toured are at the center of village life in the Ladakh.

Another Place (cont.)

Using information from the story, define these words.

1. Mausoleum _____

2. Gompa _____

3. Bharat _____

4. College _____

How old is Ansal when he visits these places?

5. Taj Mahal _____

6. Bandhavgarh _____

7. Thar Desert _____

8. Ladakh _____

Which place matches each phrase?

9. Bird sanctuary _____

10. High altitude _____

11. Tigers abound _____

12. Tibetan family _____

13. Camel ride _____

setting

What Joy!

> Read the story. Then answer the questions about settings.

Teddy just about fell out of his seat that Monday afternoon.

Mrs. Beeker, his science teacher, announced to the class that during the following week, they would go to the Colgate Nature Preserve to examine the pond life in Dilly Pond! That meant he'd be free to splash away in the water in search of his beloved leopard frogs!

When the morning of September 25 arrived, the class boarded the waiting bus in front of the school and rode off to the rural setting of Dilly Pond eighteen miles away. Students scooped and trowled for larvae,

crustaceans, and small fish. They sketched pictures of plants in and near the pond. They observed birds, mammals, and amphibians in the wetlands community. And Teddy? He mucked about in the rushes among the creatures of frog heaven.

That was thirty years ago. But Teddy still remembers. As he prepares the science laboratory for his students, his mind returns to the pond that glorious fall day so many years ago. It was the day that he first knew what he wanted to do with his life. It was one of the best days he could remember.

1. What three scenes are described in the article above?

Time	**Place**
a. _____	_____
b. _____	_____
c. _____	_____

2. What is Teddy's job today?

_____

3. What effect did the setting of his class trip have on Teddy?

_____

setting

Listen, My Children

A setting includes both a special time and place.
Below are six sound bytes. Match each with the most likely setting.

Place   **Time**

1. Boom!
    "Look, Dad! Isn't it pretty? That last one looked like a dandelion."

    _____ _____

2. "And what are you grateful for, Lydia?"

    "That I can have some pumpkin pie and turkey!"

    _____ _____

3. "All right, class, you may deliver your cards."
    "Mrs. Wilson, I made this one for you."

    _____ _____

4. "Ooh! See those flowers over there?"
    "What are those called?"
    "Well, the white ones near that big maple are called trillium."

    _____ _____

5. "You're OUT!"
    "What?"
    "You're out of there!"
    "Come on! That wasn't a strike."

    _____ _____

6. "Did you make this card, Wendy?"
    "Yes, Mom. Now go ahead. Open it!"
    "What is it?"
    "You'll see!"

    _____ _____

Places:

classroom   dinner table
at fireworks   home plate
living room   in the woods

Times:

Thanksgiving   birthday party
early spring   Fourth of July
         Valentine's Day
     during baseball season

conflict

The Winds

Read the story. Then answer the questions on page 23.

It is a cruel chill which greets us on our return to the street. Leaning into the stormy blast, Marty and I slowly advance toward the stone-faced home of our music teacher, Professor Wang. Particles of sand, dead leaves, twigs, and stray bits of paper sandblast our faces and clothes. The wind pulls on our coats, which beg to flap open although they are zipped and snapped as securely as possible. My eyes tear from the abuse of this fierce windstorm.

It is odd how utterly alone we two boys have been today. Marty received a phone call early this morning; Professor Wang wanted us to hold our piano lessons together, to prepare us for our double recital. But he could not meet us before 4 o'clock. So we were to come to his house at four and not before. We didn't mind, of course. The change of schedule gave Marty and me a whole day to explore.

I had just moved to Three Rivers in late August with my mom and sister. Marty was the first friend I'd made. It was Marty who showed me all the places to explore around town. On this October day, we checked out the marshes west of town and the old village cemetery nearby. We saw no one. Not a farmer. Not a car on the road. Not a soul. And when the wind began to pick up, I felt as though the old trees in the graveyard had come alive and were bending toward us.

The winds began to moan like ghostly spirits. Gnarled branches of ancient oaks leaned toward us as if to pluck our hats from our heads. We cut short our visit to the graveyard. Not that I'm scared of ghosts or anything. It wasn't because I tripped over a gravestone of a guy who shared my last name...although that was strange. No, nothing like that. It's just that

a bitterly cold day like this didn't seem like the best day to walk among the dead.

So we made our way down the main street a little early. No lights were on even though the steel-gray sky was as dark as dusk. We thought we'd stop at the café and have hot chocolate until it was time to go to Professor Wang's house. A candle burned in the café window. When we opened the diner's door, it pulled away from us and banged against the siding.

"Hey, shut that door!" cried Mr. Dancy, coming toward us with a towel in his hand.

"Sorry, Mr. Dancy," apologized Marty. "That wind is just too strong today."

We glanced around the dining area. Mr. Dancy had placed candles around the room. It was spooky. No radio or television was on. A couple of older men stared at us over their cups of coffee. I guess we looked puzzled.

"Electricity's out, boys. Didn't you know? I'm lucky I have gas stoves so I can keep the

The Winds (cont.)

coffee hot. Where have you boys been?"

Well, I didn't want to mention the cemetery. He might think that was just too weird. By this time we were sitting at the counter on two high stools. Marty told Mr. Dancy we were just out walking around.

"But when did we lose the lights, sir?" Marty asked.

"Just after the emergency sirens blew at the town hall. You heard about the accident, right?" We stood there, puzzled, shaking our heads.

"You better get going, boys," Mr. Dancy said softly. The two old farmers just stared and sipped. They didn't utter a word.

Marty looked at me, and I nodded at him. We got off our stools.

"You're right, sir," I said. "We'll get hot chocolate another time."

We quickly went outside and made sure we didn't bang the door too hard. When we got to the street, Marty looked back.

"Look!" he cried. "Look at the café!"

It was pitch dark. Mr. Dancy must have snuffed the candles seconds after we walked out the door. The CLOSED sign hung in the window. The building looked deserted.

We trudge on up the street toward Professor's Wang's house, against the wind. Up ahead is the rough stone front of our teacher's home. When we get closer, we can feel it; the wind is coming from his house. Curtains are whipping in the tempest, through broken windows. The door is wide open. A howl comes from inside.

We stop and stare.

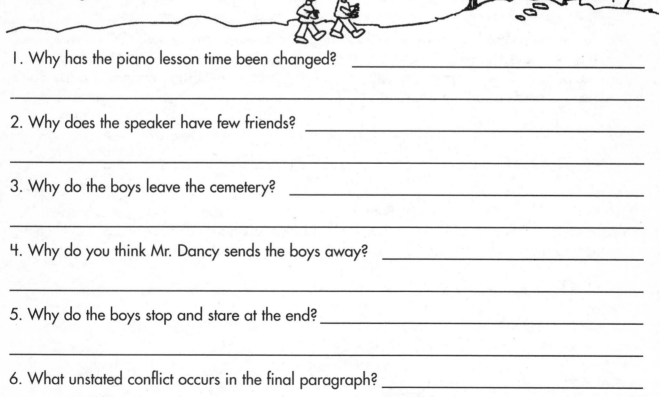

1. Why has the piano lesson time been changed? _____

_____

2. Why does the speaker have few friends? _____

_____

3. Why do the boys leave the cemetery? _____

_____

4. Why do you think Mr. Dancy sends the boys away? _____

_____

5. Why do the boys stop and stare at the end? _____

_____

6. What unstated conflict occurs in the final paragraph? _____

_____

conflict

Either Or

Below are four **conflicts**. A conflict is a problem that the character must solve. In each case below, the central character must make one of two choices. Write the two choices on the lines. Then draw a star next to the choice you think the character should make.

1. Max had a difficult decision to make. He wanted to see Tanya; she was great. But she didn't like indoor soccer, and there was a game scheduled. So Max made plans to go with Ted and Leon. Just as he hung up the phone, it rang again. It was Tanya. She called to see if he wanted to go to a movie with a group of their friends. Her dad said he would drive them.

    Either: _____

    Or: _____

2. Lee and Kip were fighting again. Not with words…with fists. Jack was Kip's friend and he knew he should stick up for him. But Kip shouldn't have blamed Lee when Kip got detention at school. It wasn't Lee's fault that Kip was late for class three times this week. Jack hated fights. Between swings and kicks, Kip called, "Hey, Jack, are you with me or what?"

    Either: _____

    Or: _____

3. Mom gave me a choice. I could go with her and Dad to Aunt Terri's house. "You haven't seen her in ages and she's always asking when you're going to come for a visit," Mom had said. Or, I could write those letters to my relatives, inviting them to my birthday party. I really don't want to do either one on my weekend.

    Either: _____

    Or: _____

4. The twins' birthday was next week. Brenda wanted the new Lollipop Land Game. Barbie wanted a Miss Tiffany Child's Oven Set. Their older sister Anna only had money for one gift for them to share. She thought they should have a good book to read.

    Either: _____

    Or: _____

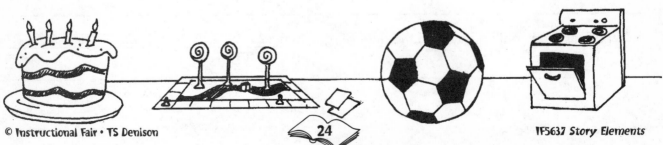

24

conflict

Who Is Bessie Blount?

Read this article about a woman who overcame obstacles to achieve her goal of helping others. Then answer the questions.

Bessie Blount, born in Hickory, Virginia, hoped to find her life's work in the medical field. This African American woman who was born in 1914 had to leave her hometown, where there were no schools available to blacks, to study physical therapy in New Jersey. She trained at both the Panzar College of Physical Education and Union Junior College. She completed her therapy training in Chicago, Illinois.

While still a young therapist, Bessie Blount saw the terrible effects of World War II on returning soldiers. She often worked with *amputees*, those who had lost arms or legs to injury or surgery. Blount's task was to assist amputees to make adjustments to their physical conditions and become more independent. For example, through therapy, she helped some of her patients learn to use their feet for tasks once done with their hands.

Perhaps we should most remember Blount's invention that gave her patients the opportunity to choose when to eat. Her machine allowed a patient, whether seated or lying prone, to bite down on a mouthpiece. This impulse would send a message to the machine, and a mouthful of food would travel through a tube to the patient's mouth. The invention gave some freedom of choice to patients who were paralyzed or disabled.

However, Ms. Blount was unable to market her invention in the United States. Why? Was it because of her race? Or her gender? Even a simpler device she created and called a "portable receptacle support" failed to find an American manufacturer. In 1952, Bessie Blount signed over the rights to her feeding devices to the French government.

1. Why did Bessie Blount have to leave her home to receive training?

_____

2. What were Blount's main responsibilities while working with amputees?

_____

3. Describe Blount's first invention to solve the problem of how her patients could eat more easily.

_____

_____

4. Why do you think Blount's inventions were not purchased by any company in the United States?

_____

_____

A Balladeer's Tale

Read the poem, which is written in the form of a ballad.
Then answer the questions on page 27.

Refrain:
I sing a song to woo my love,
Far fairer than the stars above.
I'll praise her name wherever I go,
While passing through this earth below.

(1) We met by yonder cherry tree.
I glanced at her; she winked at me.
I offered her a slice of pie.
How could I know our love would die?

(2) With pinky raised she held her spoon.
She scooped a bite that afternoon.
Into her mouth this morsel traveled,
And then she started to look baffled.

(3) She gazed at me with watery eyes,
And from her mouth there came a cry.
She gagged; she turned and ran away.
I have not seen her since that day.

(4) I chased her but to no avail,
Over hill and over dale.
You see, I like my pie with spice.
Chili powder tastes so nice!

(5) There's more of this that I could tell;
The movie rights for millions sell.
Just sit beside me while I cry…
Say, won't you try a slice of pie?

A Balladeer's Tale (cont.)

Answer the questions about the poem on page 26.

1. What conflict does the balladeer have? _____

2. Why did his love run away? _____

3. When is this poem set—the past or present? _____

4. Is this poem written in first, second, or third person? _____

5. Who are the three characters? _____

_____   _____

6. Why might you not trust this balladeer? _____

7. What conflict or problem does the listener have at the end of the poem?

_____

_____

8. Does it seem like the speaker in the poem has learned anything from his problem? _____

Why or why not? _____

_____

_____

The **theme** of a story or poem is the idea, viewpoint, or meaning which is found throughout the piece.

The theme of the fairy tale "The Three Little Pigs," for example, could be stated as "the triumph of good

over evil."

9. Circle the best theme for "A Balladeer's Tale."

   human against Nature   good versus evil   lost love and remorse   the value of friendship

action and climax

Highs and Lows

Read the sections of the story. Then answer the questions.

1   Who's to say what *you'd* do under pressure? Here's this kid, for example, blowing away, filling me up with his stinky breath! I'm getting bloated and stretched wider and wider.

a. What is the speaker? _____

2   The same nasty kid tied a string to me and taped me to a wall. There's a bunch of us stuck here side by side. Not that I'm likely to fly away. I'm not going anywhere.

b. Why can't the speaker fly away? _____

3   Great! Now another brat pulls me off the wall and sits on me. He squashes me something awful, I don't mind telling you.

4   But when he gets off of me, I stretch to my old shape...almost. Another little pointy-hat kid tries it. It's the same thing. Squish, squash. Then I'm round again.

c. What is the speaker's new problem?   _____

d. What physical quality does this character have?   _____

5   Now I've been tied to a kid's ankle. I watch others being pulled down and tied too.

6   Suddenly, there's hopping, skipping, and stomping all around the room. I hear the most dreadful sounds from my companions. POP! POP! Oh, no! Am I going to die?

e. What does he hear? _____

f. What does the speaker fear? _____

7   When it's over, I'm all alone, bruised and battered. I'm left on the floor, the game over.

8   I'm shrinking. I don't feel so tight and stretched. A draft pushes me, and I roll slowly into a corner behind a big armchair. I can rest at last.

g. Why is the speaker shrinking? _____

 On the graph to the right, rate the eight sections of the story. Which are active? Which are passive? Put Xs in the correct boxes. Then star the box that shows the climax of the story.

Active								
Passive								
Paragraph	1	2	3	4	5	6	7	8

Name _____

plot

What If?

Read the story, paying attention to the events that make up the story's **plot**. Then answer the questions on page 30.

We were settled into our sleeping bags after a really bad day.

We went fishing in the morning with Toby—after breakfast, of course—just off the dock. But that was enough. The monster of the lake pulled me into the water three times, although Toby says I'm just faking it. I'm not faking! There's a monster fish in this lake. I'm never going to swim here again...ever!

This afternoon I had archery class. I got two bull's-eyes that didn't count...just because they were on another kid's target! Then came camping-craft class. We learned how to make a stew over a campfire. How was I supposed to know the can would be so hot? I dropped the can and put out the fire. What a bunch of cry-babies those other kids are!

Well, like I said, we were just settled down in bed when I happened to look out the window. It's hard to believe any animal in its right mind would want to live in such a dark, scary place. So I was checking things out to see if everything was okay. I caught a glimmer of something big and shadowy. It was so big its

shadow blotted out all the moonlight.

When I saw that shadow, I got a little bit scared. Well, I was scared enough to poke my head down into my sleeping bag and clamp the top of the bag closed with my fist. And when Toby left us, because he wanted to be with the other counselors, I started worrying.

What would I do if a huge owl swooped down?

What if the owl smashed through the window?

And grabbed me?

And flew away with me in its claws?

Who would tell my parents?

I almost wanted to cry. I used to do that a lot. But I didn't this time. It's not a good idea to cry around other guys. Somebody might laugh.

I was getting a little hot inside my sleeping bag. I opened my fist. I popped my head out. No one else was making a sound, other than the deep-sleep breathing sounds of all the other kids in the cabin. I looked out the window.

And there it was.

What If? (cont.)

Name and briefly describe the five major events in the plot of "What If?"

1. _____
   _____

2. _____
   _____

3. _____
   _____

4. _____
   _____

5. _____
   _____

6. Of what is the boy most afraid? _____
   _____

7. How does the author bring the element of suspense into this plot? _____
   _____
   _____

8. Add one more event to bring the story to a close. _____
   _____
   _____
   _____

plot

Action!

> In each grouping below are three sentences.
> Rate the sentences by degree of excitement in this manner:
> 1 = minimum; 2 = moderate; 3 = maximum.

1. ____ Stretching itself, the wild cat ran out of its nest.
   ____ Stealthily, the cat moved toward its prey.
   ____ The huntress leaped upon its victim.

2. ____ Smiling, Sven set his bow at ease as the wary doe ran back into the forest.
   ____ A sudden snap of twigs alerted Sven to an advancing deer.
   ____ Silently, Sven notched his bow with a slender arrow.

3. ____ A motorcade made its way down our street, sirens wailing.
   ____ Fifty cycle-riding police officers protected the parade of shining vehicles.
   ____ From the window of one car, a world-famous face looked right at me and smiled!

4. ____ "Dad, may I have my allowance early this week?"
   ____ "Don't interrupt me while I'm watching the game, Hal!"
   ____ "Oh, um, I'm sorry."

5. ____ My hand shook violently as I signed the contract.
   ____ My cousin told me I was getting a good deal.
   ____ Now the Bobby Sosa card all was mine!

6. ____ Sheri's hamster was curled up in her lap.
   ____ Sheri set the hamster on the ground, letting him waddle to his bowl.
   ____ Instead of going toward the bowl, the hamster zipped under the bed.

7. ____ A gust of wind knocked Donna backward three steps.
   ____ She bent low to advance against the wintry blast.
   ____ Safe in the haven of an oak tree's windbreak, Donna shivered.

The Thickening Plot

Read each paragraph below. Decide on the main plot or story synopsis, then discover three subplot elements. Ignore any unnecessary details that don't relate to the main plot.

1.   A dragon roams the kingdom in search of new victims. News comes to the village that fourteen sheep have been barbequed by the beast as they grazed in the common pasture. Now the Lord Mayor is placing a curfew on all villagers. Gildren complains that her darning needles cannot be found. Oh, heavens! The roof of the abbey has caving in! The dragon settled upon it after a short flight, and it could not bear his weight.

Plot _____   Subplot 1 _____

_____   Subplot 2 _____

_____   Subplot 3 _____

2.   Today was a thrilling adventure from start to finish. A spider monkey ran off with my hat, and I could not get it back! We stopped to sketch the orchids, growing in brilliant colors from the trunks of the trees. While hiking up a steep trail, we heard a macaw screeching to its mate. And to finish the day, Grandma called to wish Mom a happy birthday. I miss Mom, but I'm glad Grandma and Grandpa brought me here to the Monteverde Cloud Forest of Costa Rica.

Plot _____   Subplot 1 _____

_____   Subplot 2 _____

_____   Subplot 3 _____

3.   Aye, it was hard time for us all. In the wild storm, the mast snapped. There we were with five of our crew fallen overboard and no lines with which to reach them. The *Santa Cruz* was wallowing in the sea, and we were in danger of drowning. At all hours, the men worked the pumps to empty the hold of the briny sea. In spare moments, I taught our cabin boy do scrimshaw, which is what we sailors call our sketches on whale bone. It was a dark time that I will never forget.

Plot _____   Subplot 1 _____

_____   Subplot 2 _____

_____   Subplot 3 _____

action and climax

The Gathering

Read the story. Then answer the questions on page 34.

Molly and her dad, Mike, were on their way to Uncle Don's house. Uncle Don had called all the family together to welcome back Molly and her father, who had been gone for three years. The two had lived in Cades Center, but moved away when Mike got his teaching job at Welliston College, all the way across the country. They hadn't been back since.

The party was set for seven p.m.

The house was brightly lit.

As Mike maneuvered their old Mustang down Uncle Don's street, he noticed the house was brightly lit. Although it was only Thanksgiving weekend, Christmas lights shone along the street. There were plenty of cars out front. The garage door was wide open, so people could enter the house through the attached garage. That was just like Uncle Don!

Molly and her father let themselves into the house. The family never knocked. It did seem a bit strange though that no one greeted them on the main floor. Lots of party sounds came from the basement. Aha! The family was downstairs! Molly followed with a layer cake. It would need a cutting knife. She searched the kitchen drawers for the right utensil. She also needed more forks to go with the paper plates she had brought. Mike walked over to the stairway and headed down to the party.

Molly felt bewildered. Sure, it had been three years since she'd been in the house, but the kitchen looked so different. Hadn't the sink been under the window? The new cabinets seemed too modern for Uncle Don's taste. And whose pictures were those on the refrigerator door?

While Molly fussed in the unfamiliar kitchen, Mike called down the stairs. He bounded down like a schoolboy let out for recess. Around him boomed the bass of 60s and 70s music. Ah, the good old days! When he came to the bottom of the steps, Mike greeted the women there with a hearty hello. It was odd, though. Didn't know any of them. They must be friends from Uncle Don's business, he thought.

Mike went into the next room. A foursome of people were playing cards. Mike was warmly greeted and shook hands with them. He grabbed a handful of chips and opened a can of soda.

Panic began to set in as Mike stood in the doorway of a third room and looked around. Eight or nine adults were transfixed by the latest Nicolas Cage video glowing in the television's light. Mike scanned their faces.

Mike scanned their faces.

The Gathering (cont.)

Quickly Mike spun about and raced up the stairs, meeting Molly, who was just on her way down with the cake, plates, and forks in hand.

"Turn around," Mike hissed.

Molly looked at him but, hearing his urgent voice, she obeyed the order of her red-faced father without question.

As they re-entered the kitchen Mike said, "We're in the wrong house, honey. Let's get out of here now!"

They dashed to the car, started it up, and fled down the street. About half a block down, they came to another familiar-looking house with cars, lights, and music galore. It was Uncle Don's. But their party spirit was gone. They sat perfectly still for a moment in their car seats.

Mike sighed softly. "Whatever you do," he said, "please don't tell Uncle Don what we just did. It would embarrass him that we couldn't remember his house."

Embarrass him? thought Molly. How about us? And just what am I supposed to do with this cake knife and these forks?

What about this knife and these forks?

List twelve of the central events to the story. Rate the degree of suspense of each with 1 meaning low suspense and 5 meaning high suspense or the story's climax. (Be sure to use the full range of numbers in your rating.)

1. _____   1   2   3   4   5

2. _____   1   2   3   4   5

3. Molly is puzzled as she searches for the knife.   1   2   3   4   5

4. _____   1   2   3   4   5

5. _____   1   2   3   4   5

6. _____   1   2   3   4   5

7. Mike gazes at the people in the television room.   1   2   3   4   5

8. _____   1   2   3   4   5

9. _____   1   2   3   4   5

10. Mike and Molly drive down the street.   1   2   3   4   5

11. _____   1   2   3   4   5

12. _____   1   2   3   4   5

plot and climax

Current Events

Read each paragraph below. Decide the plot or story synopsis,
and then determine what the climax of the complete story would be.

1. Kansas: A young girl, injured during the area's recent tornado, regained consciousness on
    Saturday. However, her aunt reports that the child remains confused and claims that she has freed a
    land called Oz of a wicked-witch despot. "Clearly, my niece requires more rest and possibly further
    medical treatment," stated the aunt. "I mean, she's talking about creatures called Munchkins, flying
    monkeys, and all sorts of shenanigans." The family dog escaped unhurt from the tornado and
    alerted the family to the child's whereabouts.

    Plot _____   Climax _____

    _____   _____

    _____   _____

2. Pork Corners: Mr. T. Pig and his two brothers reported Mr. B. B. Wolf to the police following an
    incident yesterday. Eyewitnesses claim that Mr. Wolf attempted to blow down the Pig residence
    by huffing and puffing. After failing to destroy the house, Mr. Wolf allegedly forced an entry
    down the chimney. "This may sound incredible, but Wolf has already destroyed two family homes
    this month," stated Mr. Pig. "He really seems to be after the entire Pig clan."

    Plot _____   Climax _____

    _____   _____

    _____   _____

3. Charming Palace: The royal family has announced the engagement His Highness, Prince
    Charming, to a Miss C. Ella of Stepmother Cottage. The engagement followed swiftly after the
    couple's first meeting at a ball held last week on the palace grounds. Area residents were
    questioned closely following Miss Ella's dramatic disappearance at midnight on the evening of the
    ball. Witnesses claim that the young woman fled the palace into the night. The prince demanded a
    search of the entire region. The search party had only a single dancing shoe with which to identify
    the missing attendee. Fortunately, Miss Ella was found unharmed at her stepmother's home.

    Plot _____   Climax _____

    _____   _____

    _____   _____

plot

Rise and Shine!

Read the story. Answer the questions on page 37.

It had all started two weeks before spring break. Spring break meant Easter eggs, candy, and rabbits. Oh, how Marcus wanted a rabbit! Or two. He made the mistake of sharing this desire at the breakfast table. Mom raised her eyebrow; older brother Al questioned where he would keep a rabbit in their tiny apartment; Lori choked on her cornflakes.

Marcus shut his mouth, deciding to keep his wishes to himself. Of course, there was no way he could have a rabbit. It just wasn't possible.

The Saturday morning before Easter found Marcus in his room. He rearranged his shelves of books, models, and building sets. He rescued a pile of dirty clothes which had been under his bed since Thanksgiving. He reread three comic books.

That afternoon, Mom took Lori and Marcus to a nearby park for the annual Easter Egg Hunt. The two children joined a hundred other neighborhood kids in a frantic search for plastic-wrapped candies hidden in tree branches and bushes, behind park benches and statues, and along the flower-bed borders.

A hundred kids searched for candies.

But Marcus felt sad. He still wanted a rabbit. He returned home from the outing twenty-seven Easter candies richer but poor in spirit. After a bowl of macaroni and cheese, he slunk off to bed.

Easter Sunday morning dawned with bright sunshine. Mom listened to a classical music station on the radio as she baked sweet rolls. Al was on the phone planning a Monday outing with some of his high school friends. Marcus stumbled into the kitchen where Mom was rolling out dough.

"Mom, where's my new blue shirt?"

"Oh. I took it out of the dryer. It's hanging in the laundry room."

The door was never locked!

"OK."

Marcus walked down the hall. The laundry room was really a catch-all: a pantry, storage closet, Al's dark room, and of course a laundry. Marcus pulled on the door handle.

The door was locked. But it was never locked!

"Hey, Mom! Why is this door locked?"

"What?" called Mom, wiping flour and dough from her hands with a dishtowel. "The door's locked? We don't lock this door."

"But it is," insisted Marcus.

He heard a sound behind the door. It wasn't loud. Hardly a thump or thud. It was more like the scratch of a fingernail on tiled floor.

Mom took down a key from over the doorframe. Her look of puzzlement didn't seem quite real. But Marcus didn't notice.

Marcus grabbed the key from his mother and slid it into the lock. He opened the door.

Rise and Shine! (cont.)

There on the floor were two large, lop-eared rabbits, pink-eyed and white-furred. And Lori was grinning like the Cheshire Cat.

"Happy Easter!" Lori sang. "Their names are Patty and Peter."

Mom smiled. "One is a girl...but we don't know which one."

Even Al popped his head in. "Hey, kid. Happy Easter! We've got a cage for your rabbits in the building garage. The guy there gave us the OK. The cage will keep these critters safe. But we should buy some feed soon."

Marcus sat down on the floor. Lori handed him a white, furry ball.

"Al and I picked them up yesterday. Aren't they cute?"

Marcus held his rabbit, too moved to even say a thank-you.

But his family understood.

His family understood.

Below is a list of eleven plot points from "Rise and Shine." Rank the events in sequential order, using *first*, *second*, *third*, etc., to put the events in order. Put a star by the event which is the story's climax.

1. _____ Marcus and Lori went to the Easter Egg Hunt in the park.

2. _____ Marcus spent the morning in his room, and read old comic books.

3. _____ Marcus grabbed the key from his mother's hand.

4. _____ Marcus had macaroni and cheese and went to bed.

5. _____ Mom listened to classical music as she baked sweet rolls.

6. _____ Al and Lori react badly to Marcus's idea of having a rabbit.

7. _____ "Happy Easter!" Lori sang, and Al looked in, too.

8. _____ Marcus heard a scratching noise from the laundry room.

9. _____ Marcus was too moved to say a thank-you.

10. _____ Two lop-eared rabbits were on the floor of the laundry room.

11. _____ Marcus decided to keep his wishes to himself.

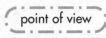
point of view

Person to Person

Below are ten short paragraphs. In each blank, write 1 for first person,
2 for second person, or 3 for third person, to identify the **point of view** of each.

____ 1. You are on a deserted island: no town, no people; just you and those crazy, noisy seagulls. What are you going to do?

____ 2. Toward the castle she fled. She begged the gatekeeper for entrance. He, an aged and faithful servant to his lord, was as deaf as a gargoyle. He did not hear her cries. Past the stone walls she scurried, the hounds in pursuit.

____ 3. Maggie bit her lip. No use crying about it. She pulled her math homework out of the sink and just stared at her little sister.

____ 4. Yesterday was not the best day to be living at our house. The dog ate all the cereal so we had nothing for breakfast but orange juice. My bike had a flat tire so I had to walk with my sister Trish. Then I found out the hot water heater had burned out, and I had planned to take a shower.

____ 5. The music is playing those lovely Christmas tunes, but you're not listening. You can't. You have too many important things to plan. What should you buy for Teddie? Who should you invite to the party? And…

____ 6. I'm not proud of it. Really, I am not. But no teacher's ever gotten through to me. I guess I'm just not cut out to be a scholar.

____ 7. When he woke up this morning, Tom looked out the open window and breathed deeply. The air, fresh and cool, made him alive with anticipation. Today was the big game!

____ 8. Columbus stood on the deck of the ship. Land was on the horizon. Land! Not the edge of the world; not dragons to devour the ship, but the land that would make his fortune…his, and Spain's.

____ 9. I think Mama forgot me. Otherwise she would come and find me. Oh, no! I've been bad! Mama said not to go see the toys because I'd get lost. Mama is going to be mad at me!

____ 10. The sky is clear. Not too much of a breeze. Perfect weather. That's why your heart is thumping, you know. It's time to do it once and for all. You've got to jump out of the plane and prove that you can skydive.

point of view

Lend Me Your Ear

Below are ten short paragraphs. In each blank, write 1 for first person,
2 for second person, or 3 for third person, to identify the **point of view** of each.

____ 1. It's true, you know? You always loved cats more than people. When you first saw…what was that cat's name? Oh, yes, Bernard! When your dad brought Bernard home from the shelter, you looked like you had gone to heaven and seen an angel.

____ 2. A domestic turkey is not a wise bird. A dog, fox, or weasel which finds its way into a turkey coop merely waits for some lame-brained and curious turkey to waddle on over for a visit. The predator has a cooperative victim!

____ 3. I don't think I can stand it any longer. I've got to tell Mom how much I dislike her asparagus custard pie. But how do I do it without hurting her feelings?

____ 4. That stubborn bachelor, Patches McCloud, had better get out of his termite-infested apartment before the walls come tumbling in on him! No one need warn him again!

____ 5. When you were born, the sun smiled down upon the earth. The moon glowed. The creatures of the night forest whispered that you, a princess, had been born to our people.

____ 6. What? You become an army sharpshooter? Why, you couldn't hit the broad side of a barn if you were leaning against it!

____ 7. She carried a large basket of laundry on her head. She had done chores like this since she was a tiny child. But this time things were different. Mkela was working at a real job now. Wouldn't her mother be proud!

____ 8. Oh, it was so dark! We will never know what caused the sudden blackout at the ballgame. We hope the game will be rescheduled.

____ 9. The song *Yankee Doodle* was used by British soldiers to mock the colonials who opposed them. But the colonists were smart enough to realize that if they embraced the mockery, it would take the sting out of it. So the song became their anthem.

____ 10. It's backbreaking work. All day long, we are bent over at the waist as we carefully replant our rice in the flooded paddy. But our feet tingle in the cool, rich, oozing mud.

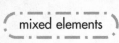

A Doomed Romance

You are my love, my love you are.
I worship you from afar
I through the branches spy you.

You, Sir, are a climbing thug.
I do not like your fuzzy mug.
Away from me, please take you!

Oh, grant me peace, my love, my dove.
Climb to my home so far above
This place you call your warren.

I like my home in sheltered hollow
Where fox and weasel may not follow.
Please go away, tree rodent!

I love your ears, so soft and tall,
I love your nose, so pink and small.
I must make you my own bride!

I will not climb, I cannot eat
The acorns that you call a treat.
Now shimmy up that oak; hide!

Now I hide up in my bower
Lonesome still, I shake and cower.
Sadness overtakes me.

I must stay on the lovely ground
With carrots crisp and cabbage round.
I long for gardens, not trees.

1. Who are the two speakers in this ballad? Identify them and write one adjectives to describe the tone of each voice.

   a. _____

   b. _____

2. In a nutshell, what story does the poem tell? Explain in one complete sentence.

   _____

   _____

3. What do you think the theme of this poem is? Write it in one phrase or sentence.

   _____

   _____

4. Circle two adjectives to describe the first speaker in the poem:

   happy   angry   hopeful   lovesick   silly

5. Circle two adjectives to describe the second speaker in the poem:

   annoyed   joyful   realistic   relaxed   happy

mixed elements

What's What?

Each sentence below has a specific purpose. If it relates to character traits, write **C**. If it extends the plot, write **P**. If it identifies the setting, write **S**.

1._____ It was a dark and stormy night.

2._____ Uncle Matt was as forgetful as ever.

3._____ She danced for hours, never knowing of the gift given to her by the green-clad elves.

4._____ "You are so mean!" howled Dina to her teasing older brother.

5._____ During the night, the clouds lifted and the moon rose brilliantly against the inky sky.

6._____ It all began beneath the smooth surface of the lake.

7._____ With a whimper, Daisy hung her head and looked at me beseechingly.

8._____ Ike knocked on the door three times, but when no one came to the entrance, he trudged off dejectedly.

9._____ The emperor's courtyard was filled with snow-white swans.

10._____ Mother's face was animated as she told us of her childhood.

11._____ Jerry met his sister to shop for their grandmother's present.

12._____ At the top of the hill was a flat, open plain with only a few gray-green boulders breaking the grassy surface.

13._____ Henry wandered into the forest to look for his lost cow.

14._____ The ungainly band of raw recruits attempted to come to attention while their drill sergeant shook his head morosely.

15._____ "Me do all that hard work? You wouldn't want me to get sick, would you?" he said slyly.

16._____ Goldilocks ran from the bears' cottage and was never seen again.

17._____ "Fido, bad dog! You get into your cage now!"

18._____ "Space...the final frontier!"

Who, What, Where?

Answer the questions for the following three paragraphs.

1.   Henry stepped out of the car and lifted its hood. Muttering under his breath, he checked the hoses and the radiator for leaks. Steam rose in thick puffs of hot, wet gas. Henry walked to the passenger's window. "Sorry, Sara," he said. "I'm afraid we're stuck here until help arrives. The radiator is low on water."

Who are the characters? _____

What is the conflict? _____

What is the setting? _____

2.   Dana hobbled over to the bench at the end of the third quarter. When she went for the rebound a couple of minutes ago, Number 43 had clobbered her! The fall was embarrassing enough, but she twisted her ankle too! She just had to stay in the game; it meant everything to her. Looking up, she saw that Coach wanted her in the huddle. Good, Dana thought. He hadn't noticed! She caught her breath at the pain as she stood. Dana couldn't even put pressure on her right foot now.

Who are the characters? _____

What is the conflict? _____

What is the setting? _____

3.   The whole class had gone cross-country skiing. We had researched the trees of our region. Ideally, each of us should be competent to identify any of the twenty-seven major species by its bark. So, when I got stumped by my eighth tree, I lost my group of ten skiers. I figured I could catch up with them by following their tracks. I figured wrong! All sorts of trails, at least ten groups from various schools, and an inch of falling snow competed to confuse me. There I was in the middle of a snowy, sylvan scene with no familiar faces to befriend me.

Who are the characters? _____

What is the conflict? _____

Where is the setting? _____

setting review

Writer's Itch

Match each genre with its most appropriate setting.
Each of the genres on the right should be used one time.

1. in the star system of Alpha Centauri

2. beneath the gracefully entwining branches of twin elms

3. at the warren of a gray-speckled hare

4. in a land beyond the mountains

5. in the abandoned mansion of the nineteenth century recluse, Thaddeus Moore

6. alone in the forest with only a pocketknife, a magnifier, and a good pair of hiking boots

7. at the OK Ranch on the ponderosa

8. at the edge of the Brazilian rainforest where farmers are having problems with erosion

9. on the Ridgewood Academy campus

a. ____ a mystery

b. ____ a romance

c. ____ a realistic story

d. ____ a space fantasy

e. ____ a western

f. ____ an environmental documentary

g. ____ a folktale

h. ____ a survival story

i. ____ an animal story

10. Choose one of the settings above and describe it using 3–5 sentences.

_____

_____

_____

_____

_____

Go, Man, Go!

Read the story. Then answer the questions on page 45.

They stretched in midfield, preparing for the morning's events. Ted, dressed in the red and white of his school, worked alongside the rest of the seventeen athletes who had come to the meet from Weston Middle School.

Theo was hardworking, and he had trained well. Since the snow thawed in early March, he had kept his disciplined regiments of warm-up, long run, sprints, and cool down. As the weeks passed, he settled into a daily four-mile run. The first few times were painful. His side ached, his calves tightened, his right knee flared, and his forehead burned. On those nights, he would flop down on his bed and sleep soundly without even undressing.

Now, on this warm and bright May morning, it was time to prove his worth, and Theo found he was very nervous. Twenty-two schools were participating in the invitational meet. The field was spangled with athletes whose school-colored clothes offered a visual display of diversity. Weston's girls had already scored points in the long jump and javelin. The boys had done well, too. Theo's high jump had won his school a second place. They also had a second and fourth in the pole vault. Not bad, considering that track and field was a brand-new sport to Weston Middle School.

Theo's main event was the 400-meter dash. It was what he dreamed of running ever since he saw his Uncle Dave's victorious sprint seven years ago. Yet, these meets made Theo so nervous, he often wished he were sacked out in front of the television instead. As he pranced about, shaking away the jitters, Theo saw a lone figure at the long jump pit. He was a thin, dark boy roughly Theo's height and build. He wore the only gray shirt in the wild mass of school colors. Even though he looked out of place, the boy seemed calm and sure of himself. Theo crossed over to the pit. He introduced himself to the runner, a friendly, determined student named Carl Alvarez. Carl was the only entrant from his school. He had taken two city buses to get there, and he was just there for the 400-meter race. Like Theo, this was his first year in track and field. Carl didn't seemed fazed by his solitary status, though; he told Theo he wanted to help form a team at his school. Returning to his own gathered team, Theo admitted to himself that Carl's attitude was impressive.

When the 400 was announced and Theo lined up, the Weston team set up a chant. Theo glanced at Carl, who didn't have anyone to cheer for him, but Carl seemed focused and ready for his race. As the pistol fired, Theo shot out. The crowded field of runners—sixteen boys in eight lanes—swarmed down the stretch. The Weston team yelled, "Go, man, go!" Every Weston student screamed as Theo's lead became evident coming out of the first curve.

Theo's heart pounded as he crossed over to the inside lane. He was leading! Footsteps thudded behind him as he entered the wide, dangerous final turn. Someone was pulling alongside him. It was Carl! They glanced at each other briefly. Then they focused. Theo looked ahead and smiled grimly. *OK, let's race*, he thought. Around the curve he ran, Carl at his side matching him step for step, yet never falling back. The two boys sped into the final stretch. Theo raced as never before, neck to neck with his challenger.

Go, Man, Go (cont.)

> Fill in the character web using the story on page 44.

Theo

Carl

personality

Personal Traits

personality

feelings before race

feelings before race

uniform color

uniform color

team members

team members

Track and Field

main event

main event

other events

other events

The setting for "Go, Man Go" has lots of detail. Find these details in the story:

1. How many schools were at the meet?_____

2. What created so much color on the field? _____

3. How long had Theo been training?_____

4. In what month does this story take place? _____

5. Describe the weather on the day of the meet. _____

6. How many runners start the 400-meter dash? _____

Answer Key

1. science fiction
2. poetry
3. historical fiction
4. biography
5. folktale
6. fairy tale
7. science fiction
8. biography
9. fantasy
10. poetry

1. science fiction
2. fantasy
3. historical fiction
4. realistic fiction

1. biography
2. tall tale
3. science fiction
4. realistic fiction
5. myth
6. tall tale

1. f.
2. d.
3. b.
4. a.
5. c.
6. e.
7. i.
8. h.
9. j.
10. k.
11. l.
12. g.
13–18. Answers will vary.

Shenee's favorite topic is graphs & charts; it was fourth. Li's favorite topic is ratios; it was fifth. Markos's favorite topic is geometry; it was first. Hanna's favorite topic is division; it was third. Tomas's favorite topic is decimals; it was second.

1. b.
2. e.

3. i.
4. a.
5. f.
6. h.
7. d.
8. j.
9. c.
10. g.

1. Francesco Melzi
2. Europe
3. "What do you know about Leonardo da Vinci?"
4. Paragraph 2: He never tired of learning.
   Paragraph 3: He wrote in mirror images.
   Paragraph 4: Much of his work was left unfinished.
   Paragraph 5: "To see" was the most important idea to him.
5. His science research
6. "to know how to see"
7. To make sketches and talk about everyday things they had seen.

1. g.
2. a.
3. d.
4. c.
5. h.
6. b.
7. e.
8. f.

1. a. to his daughter
   b. three
   c. Hannah
   d. Dad
2. e. no
   f. Jerry
   g. no
   h. yes
3. i. Michael and Portia
   j. Randy
   k. no
   l. Otis

4. m. the Utentots.
   n. Lord Vilma
   o. in the reign of Emperor Xaviar of Zelnod
   p. Trivoli

1. Ned Tuttle
2. Dorothy Wells
3. Terry
4. Lonnie Lorenzo
5. Helene
6. the deer mouse
7. Lady Beatrice
8. Steven

1. Summer after 2nd grade; camp
2. baby possum/by beech tree/ second day; sing songs/in dining hall/every noon; discover blue racer/in field/fifth day; sketch plant specimens/in state forest land/ rainy day; hear scary stories/in cabin/ bedtime; observe raccoons/in woods/one night
3. Answers will vary; campers live in cabins; they use state forest land for nature hikes; there is a lake and a large dining hall, etc.

1. b.
2. d.
3. e.
4. a.
5. c.
6–10. Answers will vary.

1. a building which houses the dead
2. a Buddhist monastery
3. the Indians' name for "India"
4. high school
5. 7
6. 8
7. 10
8. 12
9. Bandhavgarh
10. Ladakh
11. Bandhavgarh
12. Ladakh

13. Thar Desert

What Joy! 20
1. a. Monday afternoon; school
   b. September 25; Dilly Pond
   c. Thirty years later; school
2. He is a teacher.
3. It helped him know what he wanted to do in life.

Listen, My Children 21
1. at fireworks; Fourth of July
2. dinner table; Thanksgiving
3. classroom; Valentine's Day
4. in the woods; early spring
5. home plate; during baseball season
6. living room; birthday party

The Winds 22–23
1. Professor Wang was unable to meet earlier.
2. He is new in town.
3. too cold; a little scary
4. Answers will vary; maybe he was a ghost; maybe he is suspicious of them.
5. Professor Wang's door is open and his windows broken; they hear a howl from the house.
6. The boys seem uncertain what to do next.

Either Or 24
1. go to the game; go to the movie
2. stick up for Kip; stay out of fight
3. go to aunt's; write to relatives
4. buy the toys the twins want; buy a book for them

Who is Bessie Blount? 25
1. There were no schools open to blacks in her hometown.
2. To help patients adjust to the loss of limbs and make them more independent.
3. A feeding tube activated by biting.
4. Answers will vary; possibly because of prejudice against African Americans, women, or both.

A Balladeer's Tale 26-27
1. His love has run away.
2. She ran away because he had put chili powder in a pie.

3. the present
4. first person
5. the speaker, the lost love, and the listener to the balladeer's tale
6. Because he puts strange spices in his pies.
7. Whether or not to refuse a piece of pie.
8. No; he lost his love over his cooking habits, but there is no evidence that he has changed them.
9. lost love and remorse

Highs and Lows 28
a. a balloon
b. because he is taped to a wall
c. a game in which kids are trying to pop balloons by sitting on them
d. He can stretch and then return to a round shape.
e. the popping of other balloons
f. that he will be popped also
g. Air is leaking out of him.
   Chart:
   1. active
   2. passive
   3. active
   4. active
   5. passive
   6. active (climax)
   7. passive
   8. passive

What If? 29–30
1. Speaker goes fishing and falls into water.
2. Speaker goes to archery and hits another camper's target.
3. Speaker goes to camping-craft class and spills stew into fire.
4. Speaker goes to bed in cabin.
5. Speaker sees a big shadow.
6. A big owl
7. By not telling us what the shadow is; by ending the story before we know.
8. Answers will vary.

Action! 31
1. 1; 2; 3
2. 2; 3; 1
3. 1; 2; 3

4. 2; 3; 1
5. 3; 1; 2
6. 1; 2; 3
7. 3; 2; 1

The Thickening Plot 32
1. Plot: A dragon roams the kingdom.
   Subplot 1: 14 sheep were killed.
   Subplot 2: A curfew is set.
   Subplot 3: The dragon caused the roof of the abbey to cave in.
2. Plot: Speaker is on vacation with family members in the Monteverde Cloud Forest.
   Subplot 1: Spider monkey takes speaker's hat.
   Subplot 2: Speaker and companions sketch flowers.
   Subplot 3: Speaker hikes up steep trail and hears macaw.
3. Plot: A ship is in peril at sea.
   Subplot 1: The ship's mast snapped.
   Subplot 2: Five crewmen fell overboard.
   Subplot 3: Crew works pumps to keep ship from sinking.

The Gathering 33–34
1. Mike and Molly drive to Uncle Don's house; 1
2. They let themselves into the house; 1
3. Molly is puzzled as she looks for the knife; 1
4. Molly notices that the kitchen is different; 2
5. Mike enters the party; 3
6. Mike enters the card room; 3
7. Mike gazes at the people in the television room; 4
8. Mike races up stairs; 5
9. Mike tells Molly they are leaving; 5
10. Mike and Molly drive down the street; 4
11. Mike asks Molly not to tell Uncle Don about their mistake; 3
12. Molly wonders what to do with the knife and forks; 3

Current Events 35
1. Plot: A young girl claims that she

has been carried by a tornado to Oz.

Climax: The climax of "The Wizard of Oz" is when Dorothy confronts the Wicked Witch.

2. Plot: A wolf tries to destroy the home of one of three pigs.

Climax: The climax of "The Three Little Pigs" is when the Wolf can't blow down the house of bricks and climbs down the chimney.

3. Plot: A young girl flees from a ball, and is later found by the prince who wants to marry her.

Climax: The climax of "Cinderella" is when the prince searches for the owner of the glass slipper.

Rise and Shine! 36–37

1. fourth
2. third
3. eighth
4. fifth
5. sixth
6. first
7. tenth
8. seventh
9. eleventh
10. ninth
11. second

Person to Person 38

1. 2
2. 3
3. 3
4. 1
5. 2
6. 1
7. 3
8. 3
9. 1
10. 2

Lend Me Your Ear 39

1. 2
2. 3
3. 1
4. 3
5. 2
6. 2
7. 3
8. 1

9. 3
10. 1

A Doomed Romance 40

1. a. a squirrel; b. a rabbit; adjectives will vary.
2. A squirrel wants a rabbit to leave her burrow, marry him, and live with him in the trees; she refuses.
3. Answers will vary; one possible answer is "the value of knowing where you belong."
4. hopeful; lovesick
5. annoyed; realistic

What's What? 41

1. S
2. C
3. P
4. C
5. S
6. S
7. P
8. P
9. S
10. C
11. P
12. S
13. P
14. P
15. C
16. P
17. C
18. S

Who, What, Where? 42

1. Henry, Sara; they need water for their radiator; along a road.
2. Dana, Coach, Player Number 43; Dana's ankle is hurt; basketball court during a game.
3. Speaker, class of skiers; the speaker is lost; the woods in wintertime.

Writer's Itch 43

1. d.
2. b.
3. i.
4. g.
5. a.

6. h.
7. e.
8. f.
9. c.
10. Answers will vary.

Go, Man, Go! 44–45

Web answers for Theo:

personality: hardworking, disciplined

feelings before race: nervous

uniform color: red and white

team members: seventeen

main event: 400-meter dash

other events: high jump

Web answers for Carl:

personality: friendly, determined

feelings before race: calm

uniform color: none (gray t-shirt)

team members: no team

main event: 400-meter dash

other events: none

1. 22
2. uniforms from all the schools
3. since early March (3 months)
4. May
5. warm, sunny
6. 16